GOLD Wake Press

Boston, Ma

THE DIEGESIS

Chas Hoppe & Joshua Young

Bruce,
Thanks for the year
of support.
Best, Josh

Bruce —

What a great honor it
has been to learn from you,
and thank you for introducing
Josh + me to each other through
your fall 2008 poetry class. Hopefully
one day I'll have a zombie
collection in print to share
with you too!

My best,
Chas

i.

THE OPENING CRAWL

You want the past to mean
everything—
do you remember it like me

the first time you bit foil
the gas light is going the anchor
set and this moment

lulls then skids through the living
room sometimes
you can see the trash

reentering the atmosphere
the freeway curses from down
the hill you lost the package
somewhere around the bend

through you've gained an idea
but of course we can't forget
the drunk girls walking home in

clusters microbrews in corners of
bowling alleys and your face tells
me to keep it shut even

though you're just staring you
look left then right before
throwing peanut shells on

the barroom floor the partition
wakes in the tension your
confession slithers around

the dark spaces you let build
between you and the other guy

a confession

my white-boy guilt still makes me

flinch at the word *jigger*
there are four of us and the gas

is gone that's a Texas jaw we hear—
not what we hoped for
here you breath out a lazy quip

that manages somehow to define
the journey this is where they
summit and plunge—

all that booze bump and bar-talk
bleed they pulled
what they could from their

bodies and bone left hallow
and stale this is how myths are
created, right now someone's

painted *Jesus Saves* under the
overpass where the homeless go
they've put the bums to

work now you know got them
selling activist rags while wearing
sandwich boards on

street corners through the
window the city solidifies
inside the mechanical

doors are like *Star Wars*
with kinks watch
the men retreat of course

this is before the shooting at the
Jewish Center the gridlocks and
the news copters

we're solid but the present slows
us keeps us quiet *it's the coming out
that tells the tale*

and outside the jaw keeps on
there's a story in these tea leaves
to be sure

        but now

to suspend your disbelief

ii.
THE DIEGESIS

if this opening could react, it would flex and rev

when people pass. make this asphalt a part of us,

braid ourselves into its story and carry north.[1]

and you, observer, you've been pulled into the diegetic

space. can you smell the gasoline on my fingers?

can you feel the rattle of the engine? you'll get

used to it. we've been unable to push beyond

the frame, though our edits gutted the strain

our hesitations shoved into this space, and the action

smears into something recognizable. right here,

the script calls for a cut.[2] we spill forward—

---

[1] i want this silence to mean more
[2] but i'm feeling rebellious. i let it roll.

street noise. a balcony. Saturday.

the pieces come from different places you know

but right now we'll just pause on one

and let it breathe

because this one deserves forgiveness.

give four people the same photograph of this street

and ask them to crop the image any way they'd like.

collect them[3] and immediately put them in an envelope.[4]

for now we'll consider this collecting evidence,

but remind me about it later

because it won't mean anything

until we make it unfamiliar.

---

[3] but avoid folding them and cutting them into snowflakes. the point is
not that each image is unique, but that the choice meant something
different to them than it did to you.
[4] this is how i want you to think about possibility.

so, what kind of film stock are we using?

yes, we've memorized the images of who

we were at twenty, but that's only for photographs and super-8[5]

everything became sepia and musk

that pale gossip of adolescence scuttled

blacktops, circled the tether, and jigged its way into the mouths of hallways[6]

it's the coming out that tells the tale

we put a hole in the drywall

we cleared a hole in the floor and laughed into the space

inside, the darkness chewed our flashlights into pinpricks on the wall.

---

[5] i'm gonna be more famous than you even realize

[6] my brother keeps calling and i refuse to take his calls. the phone's on vibrate, and Cohen's playing, and you haven't dressed for the scene, but you strut through the frame, nines and all. i was never actually clear on the reason why this mess chugged through our neighborhood. the language gets rough around the second act. he's all sideburns and polo shirts. i haven't let go of that kind of anger. i never have anything good to say on telephones. it's all touching-base and catch-up. i had lectures planned, but they were just hot-air left over from my *Bible* days. i'm tired of setting fires to bridges and the houses above them. there are songs about this kind of meeting. but i've only heard them distorted in bar-light. the lights stringing the block flare in the lens, and just outside the frame, our mother has something awful to say.

you were right when you said *film is truth!*

the frame is like points on a map—

what happens outside

lets the focus soften[7]

can you hear that clicking from the projection room?[8]

this place is still awake.

we don't want

a digital capture,

we want

24 frames per second,

even if the sound is dirty

this is where/how lies unfold.

---

[7] i don't know what this means, but it sounded brilliant when i wrote it
[8] i bet there are poets up there capturing images—those thieves.

still on the balcony. still Saturday

that place he's standing—
about halfway between
the blue recycling bin
and the bus stop—

is not random.[9]

he's responding to a Craigslist ad
titled *someone who breathes joy.*

see how he's checking his watch?
at 4:30 he'll break into song,[10]
thus publicly identifying himself
to the blonde he thinks he'll meet.

instead, the bus pulls up
crouches to let the wheelchair off
while the man's song
is drowned out by the engine.

none of the four photographs
captured the man dressed to the nines[11]
singing on the sidewalk

but the woman in the wheelchair
told her husband about him first thing
when she got home.[12]

---

[9] we like to think of people on the street as always on their way. the act is impermanent. the location is simply a pinhole between point a and b.
[10] as per the instructions he received in our exchange.
[11] even now you can't hear him. we'll do the voiceover in post.
[12] let this be a lesson to you. there's a reason behind every crazy man's actions.

we watched the riots here

in our school's portables

but they didn't expect us

to ever learn anything.

vague memories linger,[13]

yet some of us are still

used to the substitutes[14]—

the static glass barriers

keeping us from tears.

---

[13] apropos of nothing, i no longer think the great and enigmatic figures of our planet die before their time.
[14] eventually this will have all the swear words swapped out.

our fathers taught us to speak in monologues,
all judgment and how-to.

our mothers taught us to unlisten[15]—

bless them.

      you love politics because your parents were clueless.

ooh. ooh. ooh.[16]

integrity and tennis shoes. sing, motherfucker.

it means something in this red-light[17] and black.

you won't make up your mind,[18] and in

Seattle, you bent yourself into your shirt and kept on[19]

---

[15] i've always thought of a tea party as a place where children go to make things up and learn how to gossip.

[16] i take it back you can't come over. you'll say things to lose and i'll do things to let you win.

[17] have you ever been stuck at a red light where the sun dipped just below your visor, but you were waiting to make a left turn and you knew it would turn green soon so you put your hand up to block the sun, frantically dodging your head left and right while peeking through your fingers to watch flashing red hands placate you only to realize the traffic sensors had missed you and you had to wait out another cycle?

[18] haven't i? dude, that's like my most helpless kind of anger.

[19] i'm not saying i'm right, but you're wrong.

the documentary reeks of stock footage,
proof you can parse a story out of anything.

sometimes you start listening to a song
a few bars into the phrase and can't catch up.[20]

we knew he'd met an untimely death
but the biopic only dedicates a sentence to it

right before strings introduce the end credits.[21]

---

[20] for me the other day it was *god is in the radio*, which i couldn't recognize
until the chorus.

[21] here i make the separation permanent. it wasn't what i was watching,
the Champ's face heavily shadowed in the mid-afternoon sun, his hair
mostly gone, and his voice like someone permanently clearing his throat.
it wasn't even the heartwarming speech he gave, though it seemed to
summarize everything about his legacy. it's the fallen figure, and our
inability to incorporate him into the myth in any other way than a
footnote.

it's 80s night at the 3B.
we make our bodies curve

to that beat, and when the dance floor

crushes us together, we put our hips

and lips all over each other.[22]

can you feel my hands all over the frame?

there's another flicker in the frame,[23]

announcing the diegesis.[24]

---

[22] i'm making this image.

[23] if i could, i'd flip every single light in this city on. dark always makes all kinds
of noise—the kinds you can't identify, the kinds without sources. we could
witness the scenes behind dumpsters, and what's waiting in doorways. we could
see this city takes its breaths. and if this city had an exit, we would find it near
cobblestone.

[24] i won't repeat myself. this moment is mine, mine, mine, mine, mine, mine, mine,
mine, mine, mine, mine, mine, mine, mine, mine, mine, mine, mine, mine, mine,
mine, mine, mine, mine, mine, mine, mine, mine, mine, mine, mine, mine, mine,
mine, mine, mine, mine, mine, mine, mine, mine, mine, mine, mine, mine, mine,
mine, mine, mine, mine, mine, mine, mine, mine, mine, mine, mine, mine, mine,
mine, mine, mine, mine, mine, mine, mine, mine, mine, mine, mine, mine, mine,
mine, mine, mine, mine, mine, mine, mine, mine, mine, mine, mine, mine, mine,
mine, mine, mine, mine, mine, mine, mine, mine, mine, mine, mine, mine, mine,
mine, mine, mine, mine, mine, mine, mine, mine, mine, mine, mine, mine, mine,
mine, mine, mine, mine, mine, mine, mine, mine, mine, mine, mine, mine, mine,
mine, mine, mine, mine, mine, mine, mine, mine, mine, mine, mine, mine, mine,
mine, mine, mine mine, mine, mine, mine, mine, mine, mine, mine, mine, mine,
mine, mine, mine, mine

if this moment had a soundtrack,

it would get funky, right now.

this wasn't shot in sequence[25]

and three-point lighting isn't natural.[26]

today we'll check our schedules

and block out a couple hours

before some other task crops up.[27]

we've got to get that first scene in the can,

otherwise we'll never understand how this begins.

---

[25] i promise to put the timeline back in order when i'm done.
[26] we remember everybody as a sequence of moving pictures, but i don't think all of us are cut out for the iconography of the still shot. i have a picture of my grandfather standing on a baseball field in some Navy duds. he faces the camera while throwing back a beer, his other arm triumphantly posed against his hip. baseball bats are strewn about on the grass around him, and everyone in the background seems completely indifferent to the scene, as if epic poses that capture every early 20th century American stereotype happen every day.
[27] shoestrings are better as potatoes than budgets.

our histories want to rest in the present,

but they've become bodies bending time.

everyone knows you never hit the hydrant.

you hit the curb and kept going.[28]

though we're the focus, a scene tightens till it splits just outside

our frame *that* commotion pries itself

into this space we've taken. it's muted,

but it's present. in the foreground.

do we let it stay? do we track away till it's barely

background noise like from a playground or hallway scene?

we try, but it won't be let go. it stays, it tethers to us

and claims that part of the space. if this closing

could react, it would slowly fade to black,

and Cohen, or maybe The Stones would have

laid a song to tape just for this. but it doesn't react. [29]

it's watching itself on the spool.[30] it's watching

that commotion carve a narrative inside of ours.

---

[28] someone else is to blame, i'm sure.

[29] *i won't be let go*!

[30] no, no. *i wouldn't call these miracles, just a series of letdowns*, one of us says, when the quiet swells again.

and out ahead, there are other commotions waiting

to infiltrate till we're outside the frame scraping

at the edges, scraping at the asphalt.

you've never been the crippled car on the highway,

smoke billowing from the hood as you wait

self-consciously[31] for the tow truck to show.[32]

there was the time the side window caught wind,

flapping against your Jeep until it finally lifted off

into the sunset like an Icarus running late.

do you brake for the man carrying the jettisoned

lazy boy[33] on his back down the shoulder to his truck,

or do you honk, swerve a bit,

and spike an empty bottle at him?

---

[31] most people barely notice as they pass. at most, they'll tap the breaks, their feet instinctively on cop-watch.

[32] this takes me back to the death of my first car, which got towed around the city only to end up on the lot right across from the accident.

[33] sometimes an object can be perfectly wieldy.

someone made a mess in the hall

and blamed it on the neighbors.[34]

the kids above us, are really into Waits—

Mule Variations—

and we've heard, *what's he building in there,*

at least a hundred times this week.

outside, someone painted

over the graffiti of famous faces,

but with our fingers, we can still

feel their features. we guess who is who.

---

[34] i had to. it was the only logical thing today. besides, they're the ones
always playing house music when the kids are trying to nap, the ones
sliding the glass door open to smoke at 4am, then 4:10am, then 4:15am all
night. it had to be done. don't look at me like that.

the camera settles from the treeline.

from here we can watch the neighbors fight.

sometimes, we can see them fuck.

they've learned how to be cruel.

they've learned how to cut and leave scars without a knife.

from doorways, they look like hunters in the forest,

talking about their last kills.

they'd want to carve off,

but we have to keep the secrets and capture the scene.[35] [36] [37]

they want the camera off. but we have to learn from this.

---

[35] i've never seen *Jaws*

[36] i've never seen *Gone With the Wind*

[37] i've never seen *Rambo II*

in the wreck, the car shatters,

becomes a lump of metal in the road.

our bodies were spared,

but not without slight blood loss and sore bones.

we talk about the moment like a scene.

wanting to enter it again,

dissect the seconds where change could've sparked.

so we talk and talk as though

we weren't really a part of that collision.

city lights. city lights. [38]

we love the flocks you draw.

you call us out.

---

[38] city lights. city lights. city lights. city lights. city lights. city lights. city
lights. city lights. city lights. city lights. city lights. city lights. city lights. city
lights. city lights. city lights. city lights. city lights. city lights. city lights.

interrogation rooms bulge with clues.

spin history till it meets the now.

the appearance of suits[39] blurs the line between

what is allowed and what comes true.

amputate the end of the scene.

it'll get messy and if a camera rolled it

would unhitch and shake in close-ups,

fight for focus.

Cassavetes would be all over this.[40]

---

[39] this is not meant to be heavy. but they're there with pens and paper, and they are asking for us.

[40] not because of the noir-setting. no, he's not okay with that. but think of Rowlands and Falk in *A Woman Under the Influence,* when he calls in the shrink and they want her committed, and she lets go. i mean, she takes reality and squeezes once, before she lets it fall. and when this happens the camera fights to keep in frame, in focus, as she moves, reels. i saw this is my ex's bedroom, while she was sleeping, and kept thinking, *wait, you can do that with a camera? you can let the frame get that messy?* the focus kept racking, struggling to keep clear, and even the one on sticks had to keep adjusting. that's what i mean, i mean, we won't sit still, and the suits, they want us to.

we made our way into the ether,

and let go.

we made our way into the past and disappeared.

we made our way into academia and got swallowed

up in the talk of post-colonials, post-modernism, and post-whateverism.

armor.[41]

we'll wear it if the battle escalates,

but in this rain and mud, it'd be idiotic.

---

[41] this is figurative. there is no real armor in this scene.

III.

A LENS FLARE IN THE EDITING BOOTH

MAKING THE CUT

something about him always sat
like hair an hour after the cut

it wasn't the pause for recognition
but how he couldn't settle into place

as if even the way he came to rest
was shaped by some memory

that didn't shake out with a wash.
we all knew about the before and after

even if we got the dates confused
but the tourists that drifted through

marked the differences like territory
shearing us off one by one

until he was surrounded only by people
who had mastered all the ways to say *yes.*

we called them *the liquids* for the way
they poured themselves into suits

but maybe because we blamed ourselves
for our apparent failure to adapt.

i don't want to go back to the way things were
but if i could just get back that sense of identity.

THE SKY IS FALLING

the skydiver pulled out his disposable camera

                                        you remember those

and was just about to snap a pic when a bird collided into him

and the 24-shot instamatic camera fell from the heavens

            he would have forgotten to develop the pics anyway.

✻

one time my ex-girlfriend and i were in Prescott
arguing with the windows open in my beater Honda
trying to find the freeway when we heard a ringing sound and she
flinched and either yelled or half-whimpered and reached up and pulled
a sliver of metal out of her hair and reached for her scalp to find the
blood-slicked landing patch.

✻

do you think that skydiver—like ten years later—

thinks about that camera at all,

or does he spend the time
wondering about
that poor bird's family?

✻

another time we were at Disneyland
sharing a table with some family from Minnesota.

                              i've tried writing about this before,
                                   but it hasn't worked until now

and they were having a terrible time,
or at least the dad was. he recited to us
his laundry list of this abomination's offenses—

                              the parking, the prices, the lines,
                     the walking, the heat, the noise, the whatever.
                     thank god he didn't bad mouth the churros,
                              because i would have had to slap him

—and just as he'd reached a perfect froth

a bird zipped by and shit on his bald, shiny head.

                 to this day, i've never seen a man look so defeated.

WHEN THE DAY CRAWLS

who let the grandstanders in?

their auditorium applause on
quickens this twist of bad lu

health becomes irrelevant, when blood thins
and communication flails into the space we no longer
occupy, resent spins, pitch firms, and darkens.

the why of this whole thing lacks
the kind of meaning usually
attached to these kinds of killings.

extinction is a slick thing, always slithering through crowds.

we haven't yet
become fatalists,
though the precipice
approaches. guilt
is an unsteady pulse,
rising and cresting whenever the day crawls.

CUTTING ROOM FLOOR

the
mother-to-be
is puking up
the cum shot
onto the floor
and crying
between breaths
on the set
that was made
to look
like a low-rent
living room.

now someone goes to hand her a towel.

✿

we accept these as truths:

i)   it's a hell of a thing to go viral
ii) it's not like porno ever did a good job at masking artifice, but every single piece of the machine is exposed in this shot.
iii) it took me two seconds to second-guess the claim that this scene was masturbation proof.

✿

look,
this was an outtake, okay,

but someone likes to make gag reels
of these things and sneak them into

the dvd sleeves at the Redbox
and ruin someone's Saturday night.

✻

iv) it's strange to think that there are enough creepy uncles out there to perpetuate the stereotype

✻

people won't look at me as strangely
if i say this is for a research project.

✻

oooh, excuses.

what came first, the porno or the hiding place?

CUE THE CELLOS

a steady beat kicks
above our patio, and
out in the field of
weed and blackberry,
abandoned crane limbs
and tractor scraps
artifact this forgotten
construction site.

its backdrop, the city, fumes with disgust, contracting.

so, cue the cellos—

we're in profile

SPENT SHELLS

hometown heroes
are hanging from the galleries

they look left then right
before throwing peanut shells
on the barroom floor.

      (how do you read that?

do you pause between the syllables in *barroom,*

      or do you power through them,

making the word sound more like the revving of an engine

      than the sound of the soft surface crunching against your
footsteps?)

the four-time Champ
kept a potbellied pig
that would nuzzle you
out of bed in the morning

but that was before the belts

or the marbles i found
in the gravel driveway
at his fourth of july bbq.

PUNCHING BAGS EVENTUALLY LOSE THEIR SHAPE

we all noticed it.

the champ was unusually naive
about so many things at first

that it took a while
for anyone to notice

that subtle shift of expressions
as his face collected the weight

of all the surprises
life gave him the chance to forget.

a couple of us tried to pinpoint it,
the extra weight that finally tipped the scales.

one guy claimed to have seen it,
said it was late spring five, maybe six

years ago tops, that they were
walking home, more or less alone,

and he just stopped for a second.
the guy said he'd kept silent too,

trying to figure out what was wrong
but eventually the Champ sighed, said

we took it too far tonight, didn't we?

then he laughed, kind of exaggerated,

got the other guy to join in,
and eventually they kept walking.

thing is, the guy said, *nothing
special really happened that night.*

so now i think that we'll never
realize it in the moment, that

last grain, because it's really not
like the weight wasn't building.

it's just that one day you get tired
and just let the punching bag drop,

and i guess that's not so bad.

THE TRUTH ABOUT CATHEDRALS

a sickness licks the neighborhood and blocks away, in this stone-quiet night,
                                    we hear the rusted swing set
kick into action, blocks down, from the park with the maple trees, where
                                    we used to sneak cigarettes,
and talk about the tattoos we would ink into our skin when we were old
enough.

                        we reinvented how young men
            should spend their nights, and if our parents could see this,
                        they'd still call us aimless—
            unable to see the need in the crevice of our actions.

the spread is catching its breath.

                                    this'll bring the truth about cathedrals.

            years let brick give way to plywood,
glass to flapping, black plastic.
                        what happened in there, stayed.

        silent.

        boothed.

                            unheard.

waiting for us to unwatch,

waiting to mute
                        in swathes,
                                    block by block,

till we are nose to nose,
brushing its cold with our faces.

THEE HITS OF THE RESET BUTTON

your system probably wouldn't work as well on mine.

everyone knows the blowing on the cartridge trick,
                but it was the wiggling back and forth

        that's where the real magic touch came in.

                ✿

but they only distinguish themselves right before dawn
during that brief period in the summer
when we left the windows open all day,

and
some piss drunk guy would bounce his voice off
        the walls of condo canyon

                screaming
                that's right, my dog just shit all over your pretty
                sidewalk

and many more memorable quotables
        that i swore i'd still remember

for my wake n' bake writing session when i finally got out of bed.

I LIKE YOU

sometimes
you can see
the trash
reentering
the atmosphere

sometimes
you catch bits
at dawn
and hang them on
coffee shop walls

THE RUSSIAN

have you ever seen an interrogation room without hi-contrast lighting, where shadows hung over eyelids like the upper deck at a late afternoon ballgame? cigarette smoke cuts the air. the camera starts wide—that way you can see the back of the interrogating officer—and slowly zooms in. the witness has long, greased, curly hair. his pinstriped purple button-up cradles a couple modest gold chains, and just as he's about to start spilling it he lifts his right arm, takes a drag, and props his elbow on the table so he can use the hand to gesture while he talks. just once i want this scene to play out more like absolute nonsense.

✻

does it work? frank exclaimed from beside the urinal. *i got her to confess to shit she didn't even do!*

✻

i feel like the elements exist in a simultaneous state. i've caught myself trying to explain from three different points now, and each time i realized that's not how the story really started.

✻

we'd moved back to the city. for me it was back, for her it was the first time. the new place was on the hill, and we were on the fifth or sixth floor, and the floors above us were much nicer, and our landlord had been hesitant to show them to us from the minute we walked into her office.

no, see she was going to commute three days a week. somehow we were fine with that. i mean, i know i was fine with that. this girl i had on the side, this blond chick, that's usually when we'd hang out. chick had this wonky scooter thing with a bad motor and practically no brakes, but for some reason she liked it when i towed her around town on it.

✻

but i haven't even talked about the Russian yet. he lived in the building next door. the entrance felt more like a hotel though, with a doorman and everything.

can i explain why i was there? no, and i couldn't to the doorman either. but he knew.

here for the Russian, huh? this guy was big, by the way. maybe he was more of a bouncer than a doorman. *take the elevator. corner suite to the left.*

i asked him which floor i should take, and he laughed.

✻

that one time at her place we got careless. this shit hole abutted an off-ramp, one of those windy ones. one day some crooks were driving a stolen semi-truck (who steals a semi?) and they tried to escape the chase by banking down this ramp. they took the corner too fast, and crashed into the side of the building. but this was years later.

i just remember us lying in bed, and that for some reason she got the urge to look out the window. i looked with her, just in time to see a man drop his camera and peel out of the parking lot.

✻

did i ever see the Russian?

you know, i think that was just something different altogether.

INTERSTATE LOVE SONG

do you like the way the soundtrack dates the movie?
for me this song was a drive across the state.

we liked the part
where the whole song sounded like it went underwater,

but the trip itself was lackluster
even if the memory attached to it is not.

we lose the highest pitches
as we age,

but i can still hear a tv on mute
from the other room,

and i can still see you
sticking your head out the truck window

trying to stay away while we drove home.

WE SURRENDER DURING THE SNOW STORM

we bathe in the moth-cloud, and in porch-light,
our eyes wreathed with bruises, tarred
with sill drying blood, we look like victims.

       we are not
                      mischievous,

       but our parents left us

to wreck the property behind our homes till the early snow came.

this night, we surrender, push the doors
wide and retreat into the storm.
the front of the van, tattered with rain as we revved
up the pass just hours ago, now is layered in ice

       and we cannot

       open its
              doors.

the storm kicks up again, and over the highway,
the black birds swarm in the flurries, converging
and scattered and squawking at the cold.

       we yell at them,

       tell them to

       flee.

the neighbors know her best for that time

she climbed onto the park bench on the fourth

and announced to the crowd on hand

that animals were just monsters we got used to.

so now whenever they pay her out

for babysitting their four-year-old

they never fail to remind her that (to them)

she'll always be that little girl who thought

she knew something about monsters.

THE WI-FI VOYEUR

sits two tables away
                    behind and to the right.

she's there every time you are
                    and you like to think

she says the same thing about you
                    when she gets home.

her diet's established now—
                    muffin first sandwich later

but that's surface stuff
                    and you're more concerned

with the way she snickers
                    exactly ten seconds after

you forward a joke
                    to your buddies list

the way both hands grasp
                    the cup as she peers above

her scarf at the screen
                    while you read about trends

and foreign disasters.
                    you wonder what she thinks

about your browsing habits
                    the way you read film reviews

like you have a stake in them

            or if she logs the keystrokes

you typed and deleted

            keeping a list in her mind

of all the things you couldn't say

            or learned how to say better.

OH, ARE WE TELLING THOSE KINDS OF STORIES

the murders slid over the warehouse wall,
no blood-color, just shadows meshing,
strangling the cast light. we found rituals

in the follow-through and slip-ties, knotted
in the gut, thumbing through the building
misfortunes, now tumbling into the mired

field of wires and barb. we made collages
of these frames, stacked and angled. and so,

burials became common, the cedar could
not cover the stench of laid flesh—
we topped the mounds with cinnamon

shavings and left them in the forest we
came from, leaving our histories for when
the settling is done and ready to sprawl forth.

BURN AND TURN

they always tell you to hit the showers

before they tell you you're all washed up.

it makes sense

so we won't really dwell on the thought

because the other day i learned this city breeds superheroes

and they're excellent at social networking.

i don't mind filming with handhelds unless i have to run.

*

some guys stuck a camera and a bright light in my face one night as i
was walking home from the bar
said it was some documentary they were doing.
i might have even signed a release saying
they could use my likeness.

if only i could remember what i'd said.

*

we debated on the right park bench

for him to deliver his harrowing recollection

of his rough and tumble childhood

but the tape with the piano music got jammed

in the boom operator's van

so we scrapped the whole segment.

NO TCHAIKOVSKY

he conducts the blows like her body's an orchestra

reaching the crescendo of the *1812 Overture.*

it's the way they sit at the end of it, you know?

like no one ever told them about explosions

gaining steam as they travel up the wick.

today he wheezes a question between breaths,

says, *how many legs will your horse raise*

when your followers commission your statue?

THE ORCHARD SCENE FLASHBACK

i.

flashlight beams brush the orchard arms.

we can see it from our window,
but when we listen we can not

hear voices lifting or the patter of feet.

ghosts are not uncommon around
this neck of town, but we know that

                    isn't the case—sure
                    we've heard the stories
                    our parents tell.

                    in the morning,

we search the rows, finding no evidence of the scene.

ii.

if cameras were present
they would push in on
the scene, between the rows,

claiming the light they catch,
to fill the frame with shapes
and branches. they wouldn't

shake or bump. they would keep
the focus, never blur. one take,
minutes long. just an orchard

in the pitch, little beams
of light cutting through it.
ghosts or boys, perhaps.

IT HAPPENS

the
days without a serious accident
sign on highway 2
stood only at 3 today.

later
my girlfriend
gave a witness report
to some ridiculous
accident involving
a car going the second way
on a one way street.

at dinner,
we contemplated
silverware in a soda
and farting out our mouths.

SHE'S WHAT'S LEFT OF GOOD POLICE

i.

a handful of suspects lit up the crowd
with revolvers.

overpass shadows and snow-light covers
the asphalt shattering the plane.

from rooftops witnesses can't see the flashing
light's source, but its edges crawl out from

underneath, frantic, but steady. and from
the other end, sirens pummel their way

through the sternum of this city,
coming from the hills.

ii.

the evidence room stays sealed, she cases
alley mouths, burns

through rolls of films: *press him and see what
kind of flex he shows.*

on porches, brownstone crowds and officers
make door-to-doors.

her surveillance ends in a foot-chase and a stairwell
leads to a basement and crawl

spaces where chalk lines and photographs
are made.

she walks in cradling a laptop
and avoiding eye contact.

the silence goes out with the tide
and then

hell, if i hear the phrase "man cave" one more fucking time,
i tell you
i just might goddamn snap.

i suppress the laughter
because i can tell
she's not used to swearing

(at least not anymore)
but she continues

i've unfriended people for status updates more benign than that.

she looks over the screen at me
while the cat on her coffee mug
demands a cheeseburger

i guess you can read a lot into a person's character in 140 characters, she
says

a strange start to an interrogation
—redefining social skills in this way—
but at least she was playing good cop.

WHERE WE LEAVE OUR TRACES

from the hillside on the south leg of town
where we hid

the car in the cluster of dogwoods
and cleaned
our hands with alcohol

shucked our clothes from our bodies
and bagged
them in paper sacks

we saw the plume before the fire,
couldn't smell
the gasoline and matches

                    only the burning

later, after we dress again, we will
find
the dumpster

behind the bar in the darkest creases
of downtown
to leave our traces

TRIP

all the bands i grew up with
are putting out
20th anniversary
reissues
of their classic albums

and i learn that nostalgia
only comes on
when nothing
interests me
about the present

IV.

THE SOUND TRACK

our bodies have mastered the art of knocking shit around.

chuck through our best scenes like phonebooks, flapping open.

microphone check. mic check. micro. phone. chhhhkkk.[42]

check the gate, light keeps digging its way into the magazine,

smearing into the celluloid, washing out the frame,

so all we get is mic noise and white splotches

cataracting the takes.

this is 16mm (super 16),

not the 8mm reserved for family movies,

or the 35mm of Hollywood.[43]

we shoot with what the budget allows.

film grain is natural, it coats the *real*

---

[42] i will repeat till the sound guy says *got it.*

[43] i'm making generalities here. mostly super 16mm is grainier, and cheaper, and looks pretty cool in low-lighting.

with honesty.

[subject takes deep breath] arena

the girl sat with her parents in the eighth row.
they were pretty good seats, close enough
to feel like part of the action, but still,
when you're her age, you want on the floor
so you can experience the mayhem up close.

the dad's expression didn't change once,
but mom seemed to know the words
to the cock song, mouthing along awkwardly.
can't you just see them, mother and daughter
riding along in the Subaru on the way home
from school, singing phallic metal together?

---

[44] i forgot to make the point earlier about the way no one has captured
the finite space of the frame quite the way Pac-Man has. he can't escape
the screen, and i've started to wonder if he'd like to.
[45] another way of looking at it is this: have you ever regretted watching
the *making of* of some movie? suddenly you can see the cameras. they're
right there. suddenly it all seems like such a put on.
[46] [exit, chased by a bear]

it's not like that's how people moved a hundred years ago.[47]

people didn't grind out their movements like rusted joints.[48]

it's just that someone had to turn a crank on the camera

capturing life like it was the slow moan of a *hurdy gurdy*.[49]

---

[47] while washing the dishes the coffee mug asked me *what if the hokey pokey really is what it's all about?* frankly, i'm okay with that.

[48] what do we like better: the comeback story, or the failed comeback story?

[49] i know i'm not the only one who ever asked their parents if life actually used to be in black and white.

it must be a repossessed memory.[50]

by that
do you mean
you didn't earn it
or you lost it
but got it back?

51

the bar across the street
advertises a hangover special:

a chili dog[52]
a bloody mary
an Alka Seltzer
and a cigarette.

$6.50

if the memory
still holds.[53]

---

[50] he apologizes for hitting notes that i could only reach after a full day in the shower.

[51] a placeholder (in a tuxedo (at the Oscars)).

[52] from a can on a hot plate.

[53] four years later i still get mail addressed to my ex.

people always forget the microphone is still on,
but really, we were all ready for the next scandal.[54]

it returns to you years later,
the song your roommate was playing
when you moved in a day late.

dollars to donuts[55] we can retrain you,
so please don't stop making new memories
just because you're attached to the old ones.[56]

---

[54] they promised us chin music but only delivered hold music.
[55] i had to Google this phrase. the only other option is gave me was *i'll bet you 300 dollars*, which is rather brash for a search engine.
[56] in other words, i disengaged a little from the world and snuck meaning onto its plate while i admired the flat screens above the men's room urinals.

but of course we can't forget
the drunk girls tripping in heels
down sidewalks in near-naked clusters.
if you've lived in a college town, you know.
but tonight i was walking home,
and i overheard a conversation
between two of them crossing the street
in front of me. *i'll say this*, she began[57]
but my ass has gotten way bigger[58]
since i started jogging every day.

---

[57] no, it wasn't quite like that. that phrase sounds way more like my own voice
[58] your ears perked up there too, huh?

mothers,[59]
if you keep praising every small accomplishment
we will lose all sense of the world.

in other words,[60]
this expanding and contracting
leaves us just a little shortsighted.

come back in five years
and we'll catch you up
on all the bullet points.

---

[59] journalists

[60] whilst, quiver, and the German word for candy: some of my favorite other words.

[placeholder][61] [62]

[63]

he was a film extra for about a month,
driving his jeep around down by the viaduct
until about six in the morning each day.

you ever tried to freeze frame a vhs?

she hid his parents in the gift shop bathroom
and rented a karaoke machine for his birthday.[64]

do the memories expire with the lease,
or can we stack them in boxes in the garage?

---

[61] *the answer lies in this video i found on the internet!*

[62] this here's the only place where i can be myself. that's the only reason for the first footnote.

[63] we can't say anything new about acceptance speeches, so let's just play them off. the only people offended would be the placeholder's union, but no one ever pays them any attention.

[64] i tried singing *Man on the Moon*, which i didn't know at all.

if this scene has a laugh track,

there'd be a wall of laughter and one cackle[65]

slicing its way through

you look ridiculous in those pants

and i feel stupid in this coat,

but the script girl claims continuity

shhh. shhh. shh. quiet on the set.[66]

we dug a hole in the earth behind

our house and called it a cave.

our parents filmed the whole thing.

we were thinking *Raiders of the Lost Ark*,

they were thinking *Sesame Street.*

     quiet,[67]

the set is calling, and the background is going,

so you know that means it's time to act.

---

[65] i can't hear a laugh track anymore without thinking of Jim Carey (as Kaufman) in *Man on the Moon*, yelling at Danny Devito that they were the laughs of dead people.

[66] wait for it. there's always an errant cough after a call for quiet.

[67] we also played hangman in church. mom decided god would forgive us for being bored.

we'll conflate the issues—the differences will become

what we _____ when we want to _____.[68]

man, can you smell the asphalt going back in time?[69]

i'm[70] not gonna lie, she looks like you with that hair[71]

and i'll visit that picture till it's what i think of when i heard *that* name.

---

[68] a) have . . . have nothing; b) dream . . . dream nothing; c) remember . . . forget that day; d) allow . . . want to run screaming from this place.
[69] my head was a parade float lolling first down the snack aisle then banking left to the toiletries. orange was flavor before color but blue always tastes like syrup and i'm the only balloon in sight
[70] oh it feels good to break this rule.
[71] but she stole that sweatshirt from me, godammit.

at some point
the table across from us all gets up for a smoke break,
leaving several pitchers exposed and vulnerable.
we tell him not to,
but in that unconvincing way where it's obvious
that we want to see if he can pull it off.

so he gets up, walks over, and grabs himself a pitcher.

of course the table gets back,[72] discovers the theft,
and soon the server is wondering why we're so retarded.[73]

if you pull the tabs off the top of cassettes,
you can make sure no one ever records over them,[74]

and everyone's glove box has a burn disc leftover
from that road trip they took after high school.

paper shredders could eliminate the statistics of our existence
but it's a little harder to edit out the mixtapes we left behind.

---

[72] i had to stop myself from making faces at what this chick was doing to her sandwich.

[73] oh man, and his twin and i totally threw him under the bus too. fuck the solidarity, we made sure the server knew it was all his fault. really the story ends there. it's anticlimactic i know, but i feel like i'd be really pushing your patience if i tried to say that i learned a lesson from the whole thing. it just kind of happened, and then we went back to the hotel. before that i was pacing the bathroom at some strip club, trying to figure out if i was going to yack or not.

[74] unless you tape over the holes where the tabs used to be

how many times
have you been too late to the scene
to capture the moment?

the call for *free bird* is obligatory now,[75]
a call given more to cliché
than out of an actual need to hear the song,[76]
but there's something we still like
about going through the motions.

somewhere a kid practiced all day to impress you,[77]
drank red wine because someone told him
it was good for his voice, struggled to keep fresh strings
in tune just to tumble through a couple songs
that he thought somehow approximated the truth.[78]

think about how many times this happens every day,
the lyrics sheets folded in back pockets
and forgotten before the kids even hit the stage.

it's not that we should be afraid to dream,
just that we should wonder
why all our dreams look the same.

---

[75] fucking Skynyrd. everyone and their fucking Skynyrd stories.
supposedly my mother hung out backstage with them in the 70s and
didn't smoke any of their *drugs*, and i have a friend whose friend lived next
to him in Wyoming, and they would *jam* together. i'm not impressed. and
every time i hear the song i think of tom hanks.
[76] jukeboxes always go there. can you hear the groans emanating from
every table?
[77] the easy ones: Green Day, Everclear, Nirvana, Third Eye Blind, Eagle
Eye Cherry
[78] the good songs, yeah, they mean something, but they no longer tether
to your teenage angst, whatever that was supposed to be.

he hits each nail in sideways
and places the plank by the door
because he says he doesn't trust
the shoddy deadbolt meant
to keep the outside world away.[79]

by the window at the front door
sits a cupcake pan they (she)
borrowed from the upstairs neighbors
who moved out months ago,
so the pan was retired in their honor.

it's not an instant thing,
when an object becomes too valuable to use.[80]

someone replaced the fire extinguisher
with a piece of paper that simply said *just*

just in case someone was clairvoyant enough
to get the pun in the middle of the fire.

later we'll count the smoke alarms in kitchen drawers,[81]
because no one ever thinks for a minute
that anyone's actually breaking into
the car screaming for attention in the parking lot.

---

[79] Michael Moore told me Canadians leave their doors unlocked.
[80] am i crazy to think there's money to be made selling spammers access
to your accounts in half-hour increments?
[81] five

we have aged terribly,

but confidence is contagious.

don't catch yourself when you're explaining how things used to be,
that's natural.[82]

don't catch yourself when you lose the point of the story,
a point would just seem forced anyway. [83]

take your time between songs, and disappear between sets.

take the compliments, but don't hand out any of your own.

these chords sound like questions, you see,
because we're not sure when we stopped asking them,
and it's too late to stop for directions now.

we have aged terribly.[84]

---

[82] nostaglia is brutal around old friends

[83] no, keep circling, coming back till you finish your story, and by then,
everyone's lost their interest anyway, so you embellish, slide a little fiction
between the spaces in the truth.

[84] if a *before and after* shot showed a decline, we'd lose faith in commercials

follow the surface of things[85]

it's easy from editing rooms[86]

it's easy when they've constructed space—

      wide, shot-reverse-shot.

      sew us into the pov—

but

what would happen if we plucked the sutures and held

for minutes, letting the silences rupture

the polish added in post?[87] what would happen if the camera

knocked against the table? what would happen if we

became aware of a presence just behind the lens, manipulating?

---

[85] every time she started to cry i just looked at the water gathering around the glass. i had to hide how good i felt about myself.

[86] images usually only last for two-to-four second bursts you know, to keep us from getting bored. lately we've done a lot of work with handhelds though. i'm sick of pretending the world isn't always in motion.

[87] no, i don't care how much you spent. how much did you lose?

look!

it's a trap door.

it's referring to another flick,

another moment in cinema.[88]

the diegesis gives us melody,

and we cannot hear the soundtrack[89]

as the scene clicks through

---

[88] you remember that time we muted the movie and added our own dialogue? you remember how many times later you asked me to do it again?

[89] i just got the theme from *Beverly Hills Cop* in your head.

you, dude, had marquees waiting

for those plastic letters

spelling your name, but years

on the road cut into you good,

kept you homebound.[90]

    so,

    did someone let the dying in?

    ✿

we call him a freak,[91] even though we *love* the way he dresses.[92]

---

[90] look, the impulse was unfamiliar. we're not used to seeing these things subjectively.

[91] i took a multiple choice test yesterday that asked me what a stock character was, but you weren't an option.

[92] a woman wanted for stealing a Styrofoam banana from a Wisconsin gas station while wearing a gorilla suit will not be charged.

the camera only captures that pillar of light

slipping out the roof's corner.[93]

doesn't your stomach turn when there's blood on film?

if there was a trailer for this, it would be

a series of long takes, shortening till the final shot

coasted over a bridge.[94] it wouldn't be a U2 song,

it would be Converge, spastic and shredding,

"your guitars sounds like chainsaws getting busy,"

but in the shots they all carry revolvers—

i have only knuckles and kneecaps.

through the parking lot a figure stalks.[95]

in this noir-lighting, he looks dangerous.

---

[93] alright fuck it, get rid of *should* too. i used to think you did this because it was fun.

[94] so what, there's like three guys who do voiceovers for the trailers, right? there's the guy selling family movies, the guy selling action movies, and the guy selling comedies. i think one of them died a few years ago. the other night i saw a documentary that likened us to radioactive albino crocodiles. you can't make this shit up.

[95] holy hell i'm a sucker for this scenario. i don't care if you've seen this before, you cynical asshole.

he's got

a knife

and he knows

how to use it[96]

we could argue about where the heart of America really is,[97]

but that sounds exhausting,

and pointless.

who is anchored to this block of time?

it's quite inconvenient.

you, you, you, you, you, you, you, you, you, you, you, you, you—

this is the easiest thing to say when the camera racks into focus.

---

[96] i lied, it's a prop knife. the blade retreats into the handle.
[97] just give me back that afternoon when i was eight, and the evil priest removed a still-beating heart from that man's chest. the heart erupts into flames as the body is lowered into the lava. i wonder how specific the screenplay got with this scene, and how many takes it took to really kill it.

they all carry revolvers—

who has only knuckles and knees?[98]

---

[98] i have dreams where one leg is significantly longer than the other one, and every time i try to run it just keeps dragging. this is a more familiar kind of helpless.

what

happens

when

the

money's

gone?

---

the fucker's still putting out albums, but he's been dead for years.
all my favorite albums were cut from shoestrings.

the taillights went out ahead of us.

only dust and scattering light.

those mother fucking prizefighters never lost their punch,

like to prove this in bar-light,

when the booze dug in.[101]

galleries won't hang the hometown heroes or their photos.

      in vacants we found each other's bodies

      in vacants we put up with the teeth

it's the coming out that tells the tale.[102]

that pale gossip of adolescence scuttles [103]

blacktops and circles the tether,

jigging its way into the mouths of hallways.

---

[101] there's innocence even in this, just let it trigger a memory.

[102] i like the word *point* because everything leads up to it.

[103] fuck i drank too much coffee at the Shoe again.

ha, ha. poetry?

that's an excuse to rummage through

old images, and film's an excuse to bend time.

we love Godard because he's a prick,[104]

but also because he blurs the line[105] between

fiction and truth.

i'm looking for the freeway, but i keep

ending up in cul-de-sacs,[106]

can you tell me how to get to the college?[107]

---

[104] give me Herzog.

[105] how soon were you ready to leave after you first sat down?

[106] someone told me the first hidden track ever was on *Sgt. Pepper*. In comes a shrill voice (i assume Paul, that attention whore) saying something like *never could be any other way* over and over, and underneath that there's chatter, because really there always is, and then even underneath there's someone else (i assume John because he hated to be one-upped by whorish Paul) going *bah ba ba ba da da*. It's on the cd too, but it's meant to loop on the record's final groove. some illusions don't transfer.

[107] some allusions don't transfer.

look, if you give me coffee, i can keep going,

but these desperation tentacles are tightening.[108]

and, wait, wait, wait, if you quiet down

you can hear that click, click, clicking

coming from over *there,* where the frame is.

---

[108] stay past the credits this one time.

V.
THE CREDITS

This is for adults we're kerfed the
light just enough to keep us
going given a binary people

like you always complete the
circuit instead of walking away
Cassavetes Cassavetes your

ghost is pummeling in my chest
men cling to stalls and i want the
camera to rack but they

shuck meaning onto my plate
while i read the paper above the
urinal no it's touch

            and

there's good solid fucking
evidence behind the picture
frames i can still hear the wind

beating against the truck's open
windows as we tried to stay
awake on the drive home take

the venom flossing the peaks at
sunrise use it to blow out the lens
from here we can agree

that we can't fly when someone
else is watching this is what you
were built for and that kind

of anger (frustration) likes to
bite when the weather gets spotty
like marbles i found in

the driveway at the fourth of july
barbeque and when things got
real bad everyone draped

blankets over the front windows
of houses—smoke and laughter
you know

*how do you know if this sanitizer
keeps you from getting sick* in the
bathroom the light flickers film-like

this is cinema this is what
Goddard would shoot

but the song

that's just something they stuck
in for cross promotion and
product placement

Joshua Young is the author of *When the Wolves Quit: A Play-In-Verse* (Gold Wake Press) and *To the Chapel of Light* (Mud Luscious Press/Nephew). He lives in Chicago with his wife, their son, and their dog. For info about his writing, films, and other projects visit http://thestorythief.tumblr.com

Chas Hoppe pays bills as a writer and editor, and pays respect through music and poetry. Some of his poems can be found in *Alligator Juniper, Glass,* and *Jeopardy.* This is his first full-length poetry collection, and he's grateful to the juggernaut known as Joshua Young for inviting him along for the journey. Follow Chas's exploits at www.chashoppe.com.

Acknowledgements:

Hi-fives to the Faculty at Western Washington University, especially Bruce Beasley, Oliver de la Paz, Brenda Miller, Kaveh Askari, Doug Park, and Kathryn Trueblood, whose classes informed this book in so many ways and introduced us to each other. Hi-fives to our friends and families. Hi-fives and other things to our signifs: Amanda & Emily. Hi-fives to Elliot. Hi-fives to Jared and Gold Wake Press. Hi-fives to the journals who took pieces from this beast: elimae, Gold Wake echaps, and Heavy Feather Review. Hi-fives to Matt & Chelsea for the years of film theory discussion, among other things. Hi-fives to our B'ham friends, just 'cause. Hi-fives to the folks (faculty and cohort) at Columbia College—Holy shit, you are supportive! Hi-fives to Michael Robins, Gregory Sherl, & Jenny Boully. Hi-fives to you for reading this. Thank you.

CPSIA information can be obtained at www.ICGtesting.com
Printed in the USA
BVOW032052230113

311447BV00001B/2/P